Text and photographs © 2015 by The Taunton Press, Inc.

Text: Charlotte Styles
Jacket/Interior design: Kimberly Adis
Interior layout: Kimberly Shake
Photographer: Alexandra Grablewski
Executive editor, Series: Shawna Mullen
Assistant editor, Series: Timothy Stobierski
Series art director: Rosalind Loeb Wanke
Series production editor: Lynne Phillips
Copy editor: Candace B. Levy

The Taunton Press
Inspiration for hands-on living®

The Taunton Press, Inc., 63 South Main Street,
PO Box 5506, Newtown, CT 06470-5506
e-mail: tp@taunton.com

Threads® is a trademark of The Taunton Press, Inc.,
registered in the U.S. Patent and Trademark Office.

The following names/manufacturers appearing in
Tie–Dye and Bleach Paint are trademarks: Clorox®,
Jo-Ann Stores℠, Michaels®, Tulip®, Walmart®

Library of Congress Cataloging-in-Publication Data
in progress

ISBN # 978-1-62710-989-5

Printed in the United States of America
10 9 8 7 6 5 4 3 2 1

contents

techniques

Looking for an inexpensive way to give clothing and other items a personal touch? Tie–dye and bleach offer two different, but in many ways similar, options. One involves adding color, while the other is about removing color to create unique patterns.

Tie–dye has been around for centuries, but we tend to think of it as emerging from the hippie movement of the 1960s. Back then the style was to add as many colors as possible to create a vibrant swirl. Today, simple designs and a subdued palette are more fashionable. So choose a look you like and get started! Soon you'll be sporting one-of-a-kind creations that you'll be proud to say you made yourself.

Note: Before beginning a tie–dye project, it's important to launder your item to remove any fabric finishes and improve how the item will absorb the dye. Then follow the steps given next to achieve the style you want.

SIMPLE CIRCLE

Pinch the item in the center and wrap with a rubber band. The circle you create will have a diameter twice as big as the distance between the pinched center and the rubber band. Dip the pinched end in your dye for a colored circle, or the ends for a white circle with a colored border.

ACCORDION PLEAT FOLD

Fold the sleeves in and the neck and shoulders down to create a rectangular shape. Turn the T-shirt right side up. Starting at the top of the shirt, fold approximately 2 in. of the shirt down, then fold the next 2 in. under the shirt, accordion style. Fold the next 2 in. over the shirt again, and continue this way until you get to the bottom of the shirt. Smooth out wrinkles as you work. Holding one end of the folded shirt, start folding in the opposite direction: Fold about 2 in. over the shirt, then fold the next 2 in. under the shirt. Continue folding this way to the end of the shirt. Using wide rubber bands spaced equally, bind the accordion-folded T-shirt twice along the width and twice along the length.

REMEMBER!

Whether you're bleaching or dyeing, always remember that you'll want to work in a space with plenty of ventilation. If you can do your project outdoors, that's the best. If not, make sure that you open all the windows and turn on a fan.

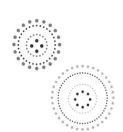

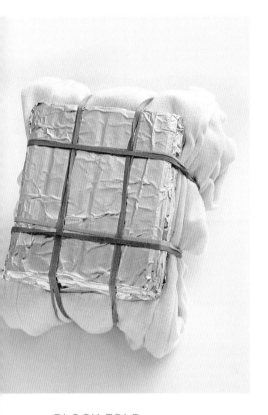

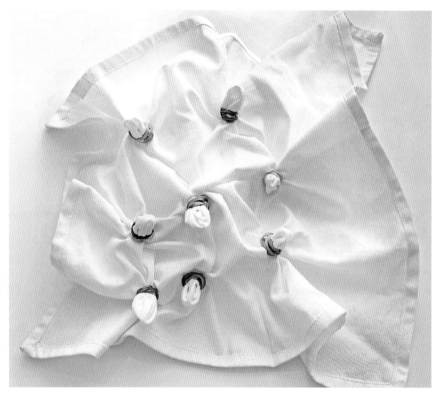

BLOCK FOLD

Follow the same instructions as for the "Accordion Pleat Fold." Cut two rectangles out of cardboard, about 1 in. smaller in length and width than the bundle. Cover each piece of cardboard in foil. Sandwich the bundled T-shirt between them, using two wide rubber bands in each direction.

TINY BUNDLES

Gather a small bunch of fabric and wrap with a narrow rubber band. Repeat over the front and back of the garment.

TIP When you are finished dyeing your fabrics, rinse them with cool water in a sink or tub until the water runs clear. Then wash the material on its own in a washing machine. You may want to do this for several cycles to ensure that any remaining dye does not stain other clothes. Use Synthrapol or another dye–fixing detergent for any tie–dye project that will regularly washed.

BLEACH

For bleach crafts, use any liquid chlorine bleach or bleach pen (do not use nonchlorine or powdered bleach). Always choose fabrics made of all-natural fibers, like cotton, for bleach projects. When working with a bleach pen, it can take a few minutes for your design to show up, so work slowly and wait to see what you've got before moving on.

Because bleach can damage fibers, once you've achieved the effect you're going for, you'll want to neutralize it. This can be done by pouring hydrogen peroxide over the item or using a neutralizer such as Bleach-Stop.

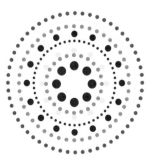

Bleach-Dipped Pillow

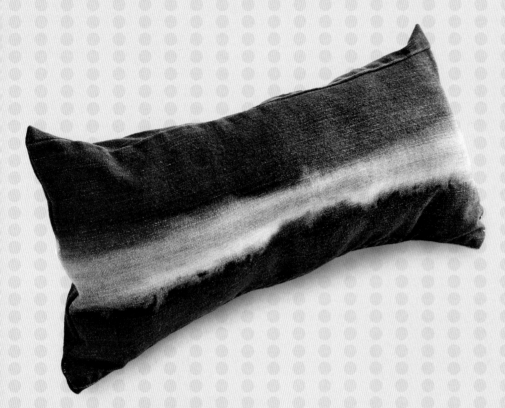

Using this technique of dipping denim in bleach, you can create interesting, varied designs. Use the leg of an old pair of jeans, and with two short seams, you've got a pillow!

SKILL LEVEL

Intermediate

MATERIALS

Rubber gloves

Measuring cup

Bleach

Rectangular baking pan

Stir stick

Scissors

Pair of straight-legged jeans

Bucket

Hydrogen peroxide

Needle and thread

Fiberfill stuffing

TO MAKE THE PILLOW

1. Wearing rubber gloves, measure 1 cup bleach and 1/2 cup water and pour the solution into a baking pan. Stir. Cut the leg off of a pair of jeans, then trim it so that it measures approximately 17 in. long. Be sure to select the straightest portion of the leg (the part with the least amount of flare).

2. Fold the pant leg in half lengthwise, then in half again widthwise. Dip the folded edge of the pant leg into the bleach solution, immersing only about 1/2 in. or less of the denim, and hold it there for about 5 minutes or until the dipped portion turns white.

3. Unfold the pant leg and immerse it in a bucket of cold water for 10 minutes. Rinse. Pour hydrogen peroxide over the bleached portion. Let it sit for 10 minutes and then rinse; machine-wash the denim and dry. Turn the pant leg inside out. Sew one end closed, using a 1/2-in. seam allowance. Sew the other end halfway, then turn the leg right-side out. Stuff the pillow with fiberfill and finish sewing the seam.

TIP Try to hold the jeans as level as possible while dipping them in the bleach so the resulting line will be straight, too.

Tie-Dye Shoes

Make these bright, colorful kicks using permanent markers. You can also use this technique on a baseball cap.

SKILL LEVEL
Beginner

MATERIALS
Cotton rag

Permanent markers in a variety of colors (yellow, light green, orange, pink, purple)

Cloth shoes in white

Rubbing alcohol

Dropper

TO MAKE THE SHOES

1. Practice drawing starbursts on a cotton rag. Experiment with mixing colors, such as orange and pink. Draw several starbursts—a circle of lines that intersect in the center—near one another, then fill in the empty space with yellow. Using a dropper, drop rubbing alcohol on the design to make the colors run. Do this slowly, drop by drop, because this helps achieve a more blended design.

2. When you're ready, repeat the previous step on the shoes. Be careful not to use too many dark colors, which can overpower an otherwise bright design.

TIP Once you see the design you've created, you can go back and add more color, followed by a few more drops of rubbing alcohol.

Spray-Bleach Tote Bag

Use this easy technique to create a cool splatter effect. Try it on T-shirts, cotton jersey dresses, sweat pants, or pretty much anything! Want stripes? Use a bottle with a steady stream and squirt in a continuous line.

SKILL LEVEL

Beginner

MATERIALS

Rubber gloves

Bleach

Spray bottle

Corrugated cardboard

Colored tote bag (made of natural fibers)

Hydrogen peroxide

TO MAKE THE BAG

1. Wearing rubber gloves, pour about 1 cup of bleach into a spray bottle. To prevent the bleach from soaking through to the other side of the bag, put several pieces of corrugated cardboard inside the bag.

2. Find a place to work where the floors and walls won't be harmed by bleach. A tile shower stall is a good option; outdoors is even better—*but only on a calm day* (a strong breeze could blow the spray back at you). Hang the bag. Holding the spray bottle about 1 ft. from the bag, spray the bag with bleach once, then wait to see how the splatter appears. Spray a second time, again waiting for the fade marks to appear. Continue this way until you're satisfied with the results. (I sprayed the bag shown only four times.)

3. Remove the cardboard. To neutralize the bleach, place the bag face up in a bowl or on the bottom of the bathtub or on an outdoor concrete surface and pour hydrogen peroxide over it. Let it sit for about 15 minutes, then rinse with water. Launder before using.

TIP When working with bleach spray, you need to be careful not to get any bleach on the clothing that you're wearing, as it will fade and discolor upon contact. It's best to not wear any favorites when you're using bleach; wear the kind of clothes you would paint a room or do yard work in.

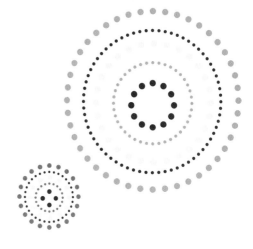

Doodle Shoes

Transform an ordinary pair of cloth shoes into a work of art, using your own signature doodle style.

SKILL LEVEL
Intermediate

MATERIALS
Pen
Scrap paper
Chalk
Cloth shoes
Bleach pen
Saucer or small bowl
Fine-tip paintbrush
Hydrogen peroxide
Spray bottle

TO MAKE THE SHOES

1. Start by sketching out your ideas on scrap paper. When you are satisfied with the design, draw it on the shoes in chalk.

2. Squeeze the contents of the bleach pen into a saucer or bowl. Use the paintbrush to paint on the design. Go back and forth between the left and right shoe, doing a little bit on one and then switching to the other. This allows time for the design to appear. Continue this way until both shoes are finished.

3. Let the shoes sit for 1 hour or so, then rinse thoroughly in cold water. Pour about 1 cup of hydrogen peroxide into the spray bottle and spray the shoes. Let sit for several hours, then rinse again.

> **TIP** Some fabrics are more porous than others. Test the fabric of the shoes by making a dot with the bleach pen in an inconspicuous spot. If the dot bleeds a lot, the shoes aren't good candidates for this project.

Tie-Dye Napkins

Turn plain white napkins into something special. Make an extra set to give as a gift!

SKILL LEVEL

Intermediate

MATERIALS

White cotton napkins (20-in. square)

Wide rubber bands

Plastic wrap

Rubber gloves

Dye

Bucket, about 18 in. tall

Stir stick

Thin dowel rod

Clothespins

Dye fixative or dye-fixing detergent

TO MAKE THE NAPKINS

1. Pinch a napkin in its center, then wrap a wide rubber band around it (see the "Simple Circle" photo, p. 4). Cover the fabric below the rubber band in plastic wrap, then add a second rubber band over the first (to hold the plastic wrap in place). Trim the edges of the plastic wrap close to rubber band. Wet the portion of the napkin above the rubber bands with water. Repeat for each napkin.

2. Wearing gloves, prepare the dye in a plastic bucket, following the manufacturer's instructions. Make sure that the dye is 10 in. to 11 in. deep in the bucket.

3. Place the dowel over the bucket and use a clothespin to hang the napkins upside down from it so that the portion without the plastic wrap is immersed in the dye. Hang as many napkins as will fit (probably two or three). Let the napkins soak in the dye for 25 to 30 minutes, or until they reach the desired color; stir the dye frequently (refer to the manufacturer's instructions).

4. Remove the napkins from the dye and rinse in water. Use a dye fixative or launder with dye-fixing detergent.

Accordion Fold T-Shirt

Have fun choosing a pretty color combo for this project. The accordion fold technique uses negative space to really give your shirt an interesting look—the areas lacking dye are an integral part of what makes this shirt fun. Choose a pretty color combination, like the blue and purple used here, for a shirt you won't ever want to take off!

SKILL LEVEL

Intermediate

MATERIALS

White T-shirt
Rubber bands
Rubber gloves
Dye, two colors
2 squeeze bottles
Plastic bag
Dye fixative or dye-fixing detergent

TO MAKE THE T-SHIRT

1. Dampen the T-shirt with water and arrange it, face down, on a flat surface.

2. Fold the shirt as directed in "Accordion Pleat Fold" on p. 4. Smooth out the wrinkles as you work.

3. Prep the workspace. Wearing rubber gloves, prepare the dyes according to the manufacturer's instructions and pour them into the squeeze bottles.

4. Saturate the outer portion (about one-third of the bundle on each side) with color A and saturate the middle portion with color B. Place the T-shirt in a plastic bag and let it sit for 2 to 3 hours.

5. Remove the T-shirt from the bag and undo the rubber bands. Let the shirt dry.

6. To set the dye, apply a dye fixative or launder the T-shirt with a dye-fixing detergent.

TIP This technique works well on shirts with long sleeves, but there's no reason you couldn't just use a standard short-sleeved tee or even a pair of leggings. Have fun experimenting!

Block Tie-Dye T-Shirt

This is another technique that makes great use of white space (there may actually be more white on the shirt than there is color!). Using a block gives the shirt a really crisp design, leaving more of the shirt blank to achieve some interest through contrast.

SKILL LEVEL

Intermediate

MATERIALS

White T-shirt

Wide rubber bands

Cardboard

Scissors

Aluminum foil

Rubber gloves

Dye, two colors

2 squeeze bottles

Plastic bag

Dye fixative or dye-fixing detergent

TO MAKE THE T-SHIRT

1. Dampen the T-shirt with water and arrange it, face down, on a flat surface.

2. Fold the shirt as directed in "Accordion Pleat Fold" on p. 4. Smooth out the wrinkles as you work.

3. Cut two squares or rectangles, slightly smaller than the folded T-shirt, out of stiff cardboard. Tightly wrap each piece in foil. Sandwich the T-shirt between the pieces of cardboard.

4. Using four wide rubber bands, secure it twice each way (as shown on p. 5)

5. Prep the workspace. Wearing rubber gloves, prepare the dyes according to the manufacturer's instructions and pour them into the squeeze bottles.

6. Saturate the outer portion (about one-third of the bundle on each side) with color A, and saturate the middle portion with color B. Place the T-shirt in a plastic bag and let sit for 2 to 3 hours.

7. Remove the T-shirt from the bag, undo the rubber bands, and remove and discard the cardboard. Let the shirt dry.

8. To set the dye, apply a dye fixative or launder the T-shirt with a dye-fixing detergent.

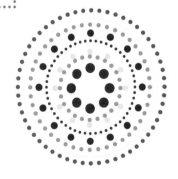

Splatter Tank Top

There's nothing worse than spilling dye on one of your favorite shirts. If you happen to get some color on a white shirt, why not make the spill a part of the design? Splatter your dye onto the shirt and cover up any imperfections. Let your creativity run wild with this fun-to-make, fun-to-wear project.

SKILL LEVEL
Beginner

MATERIALS
White tank top
Rubber gloves
Dye, two colors
2 squeeze bottles
Drying rack
Plastic wrap
Dye fixative or dye-fixing detergent

TO MAKE THE TANK

1. Prep the workspace. Dampen the tank top with water and lay it flat on the work surface.

2. Wearing rubber gloves, prepare the dyes according to the manufacturer's instructions and pour them into the squeeze bottles.

3. Drip the first dye across the tank top, working in diagonal slashes. Apply dye more heavily at the bottom and lighter at the top.

4. Using the second color, drip the dye across the tank top, working in diagonal slashes.

5. Place the tank top flat on a drying rack. Cover with plastic wrap and let sit for 2 to 3 hours. Remove the plastic and let the tank dry.

6. To set the dye, apply a dye fixative or launder the tank with a dye-fixing detergent.

TIP You don't have to start with a white top—try a shirt in some other pale color, then choose colors of dye that coordinate with it. A mellow yellow shirt splattered with some greens and reds can look really great!

Indigo Tote Bag

This classic shade is everywhere right now. Jump on the trend with a swinging bag.

SKILL LEVEL

Beginner

MATERIALS

Plain white tote bag

Wide rubber bands

Rubber gloves

Dye in indigo or denim blue

Bucket or pot (depending on dyeing technique you plan to use)

Stir stick

Dye fixative or dye-fixing detergent

TO MAKE THE BAG

1. Dampen the bag with water. Pinch the bag in the center and wrap with a rubber band (see the "Simple Circle" photo on p. 4), about two-thirds of the way between the pinched center and the edges. Add several more rubber bands here, which will make the white ring in the design.

2. Prep the workspace. Wearing rubber gloves, prepare the dye according to the manufacturer's instructions. Immerse the bag in the dye bucket and let sit for 20 to 30 minutes (or according to the manufacturer's instructions), stirring occasionally.

3. Remove the tote from the dye and let it sit overnight. Remove the rubber bands and rinse the tote in cold water. Apply a dye fixative or wash the bag in a dye-fixing detergent.

TIP Dark-colored dyes can rub off onto your clothes, so before using this bag, it's best to wash it several times.

Camouflage Leggings

Who says that camouflage is for blending in? These cute leggings will make you stand out, in the best possible way!

SKILL LEVEL
Intermediate

MATERIALS
White leggings
Rubber bands
Rubber gloves
Dye, in four colors: yellow, light green, dark green, and brown
4 squeeze bottles
Plastic bag
Dye fixative or dye-fixing detergent

TO MAKE THE LEGGINGS

1. Prep the workspace. Dampen the leggings with water and lay flat on the work surface. Gather a small bunch of the fabric and wrap it with a rubber band. Repeat over the front and back of the leggings (see "Tiny Bundles" technique on p. 5). Wearing rubber gloves, prepare the dyes according to the manufacturer's instructions and pour each color into a squeeze bottle.

2. Drizzle one color at a time over the leggings, saving the color you want to be most noticeable for last. Try to keep the colors distinct.

3. Place the leggings in a plastic bag and let sit for 5 hours or more, so the colors saturate. Remove the leggings from the bag and rinse in cool water until the water runs clear. Remove the rubber bands. To set the dye, apply a dye fixative or launder the leggings in a dye-fixing detergent.

TIP Camouflage not your thing? These look great in any color combo! Try three different shades of blue or red for an awesome flair.

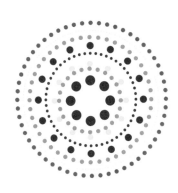

Dip-Dye Scarf

Get that boho chic look the cheap and easy way. Just buy any old white scarf and have at it. Or, you can do what I did and cut up some T-shirts for a fast, fun, inexpensive scarf. This is one bit of tie–dye you'll be happy to wear in all seasons.

SKILL LEVEL
Beginner

MATERIALS
Large white T-shirt or white cotton scarf

Scissors

Rubber gloves

Dye, 2 colors

2 plastic bins

Dye fixative or dye-fixing detergent

TO MAKE THE SCARF

1. Lay the T-shirt flat on the work surface. Cut straight across the shirt, just under the sleeves. Discard the top portion (the part with the sleeves).

2. Cut one side to create a long scarf, or leave intact for an infinity scarf. Trim to the desired width.

3. Prep the workspace. Wearing rubber gloves, prepare the dyes in the plastic bins according to the manufacturer's instructions. (For this project, don't use the stovetop method explained in the manufacturer's instructions.)

4. Dampen the scarf with water. Fold horizontally, accordion-style, making each fold about 5 in. wide.

5. Dip one side of the folded bundle into the lighter color of dye, immersing it to half the size of the stripe that you want (for instance, if you want a 3-in. stripe, dip it 1$\frac{1}{2}$ in.). Hold the scarf in the dye until it reaches the desired shade.

6. Holding the dyed edge in gloved hands, dip the opposite side of the folded bundle in the darker color, following the instructions in Step 5.

7. Rinse the scarf in cold water until the water runs clear. To set the dye, apply a dye fixative or launder the scarf in a dye-fixing detergent.

8. Are two colors just not enough? If so, rinse the scarf until the water runs clear, set the dye, and let the scarf dry. You can then refold the scarf so that you can dip the white edges into a new color. Try thin strips for some real style!

TIP For this project, the bigger the T-shirt, the better—look for size XXL or XXXL.

Aztec-Style Jeans

Customize an ordinary pair of jeans using bleach and a permanent marker. I chose to do mine in an Aztec style because I love the sharp geometric lines that the pattern creates. But that's not the only civilization you can look to for inspiration: Ancient Greece, Rome, Egypt, and Asia all have interesting patterns and motifs that you can use to create really one-of-a-kind jeans!

SKILL LEVEL

Intermediate

MATERIALS

Measuring cup

Bleach

Bucket

Stir stick

Jeans

Dowel rod

Hydrogen peroxide

Scrap paper

Pencil

Ruler

Permanent black markers, fine and ultra-fine points

TO MAKE THE JEANS

1. Mix 2 cups bleach and 1 cup water in a bucket and stir until you are confident that the solution is well-mixed.

2. Dip the bottom of each leg of the jeans (5 in. to 6 in.) in the bleach solution. Lay the dowel over the top of the bucket and drape the jeans over it so the bottoms can soak.

3. Let the jeans soak for 15 minutes; if they aren't light enough, leave them for another 5 minutes. Keep checking in 5-minute intervals until you're happy with the color.

4. Rinse the jeans in cold water. Empty the bucket and clean it thoroughly with soap and water. Put the bleached part of the jeans back in the bucket and pour hydrogen peroxide over them.

5. Let them soak in the hydrogen peroxide for 15 minutes. Rinse again and launder the jeans.

6. Do an Internet search for Aztec designs. Sketch your design ideas on paper. When you've developed a design you like, mark it out on the jeans using a pencil and a ruler.

7. Fill the design in with the markers. Doodle as much or as little as you like to achieve either a subtle pattern or an all-out fashion statement.

TIP I made this pair by bleaching the bottoms of the legs, but you can have all kinds of fun with this technique once you're comfortable with it. Try bleaching the waistband next time and filling it with your design, or really kick things up a notch by using the technique on both the waist and the legs.

Ombré Floral Pillowcase

Are your pillows so boring to look at that they're putting you to sleep? You can update an old pillowcase fast and easily with this fun technique. I used a floral pattern, but the technique works just as well on other designs—anchors, seashells, solid colors—try whatever gets you happy!

SKILL LEVEL
Beginner

MATERIALS
Measuring cup
Bleach
Bucket
Stir stick
Floral patterned pillow case, 100 percent cotton
Hydrogen peroxide

TO MAKE THE PILLOWCASE

1. Mix a solution of 2 cups water and 1 cup bleach in a bucket. Stir to blend.

2. Fold the pillowcase in half. Dip the fold into the solution, about 1/2 in. deep.

3. Hold for 1 or 2 minutes, then lower the already bleached end 1/2 in. deeper into the bleach solution and let soak for 1 or 2 minutes. This is what creates the gradual fade characteristic of an ombré design. Unfold the pillowcase.

4. To make a parallel stripe, dip one edge of the pillowcase in the bleach solution, letting 1/2 in. soak for 1 or 2 minutes. Then lower the already bleached end 1/2 in. deeper into the bleach solution and let soak for 1 or 2 minutes.

5. Repeat Step 4 for the opposite edge.

6. Remove the pillowcase from the bleach solution. Rinse in water, then pour hydrogen peroxide over the pillowcase.

7. Let it soak for 15 minutes, then rinse again. Launder.

TIP Have some pretty fabric that you're not using? Use this technique to dip-dye it, then sew it into café curtains, napkins, or a tote.

Flower Pillowcase

Use a paintbrush and dye to create this pop art–style blossom. You don't need to be an artist to get great results! If you're worried that you might not have the skills to do this freehand, just buy a stencil in the design that you want and you can achieve the same results!

SKILL LEVEL

Beginner

MATERIALS

Rubber gloves

Dye in three colors: yellow, pink, dark purple

3 bowls

Plain white pillowcase

Paintbrushes: a medium watercolor brush, a flat 1-in. brush, and a small round brush

TO MAKE THE PILLOWCASE

1. Prep the workspace. Wearing rubber gloves, mix the dyes according to the manufacturer's instructions. Pour a small amount of each color into its own bowl.

2. Using the medium watercolor paintbrush, dab yellow dye in a roughly 2-in. circle off-center to the upper right.

3. Using the same brush, paint rough strokes in pink to form the petals' base, starting a few inches away from the yellow center and brushing inward. Using the same brush will let the colors mix and create some pretty shades.

4. Using the 1-in. paintbrush, paint full pink petals, extending almost to the edge of the pillow.

5. Dip the same brush in the dark purple dye. Paint a dark edge around the end of each petal, brushing inward, so the purple extends into the pink.

6. Using the small paintbrush, paint several small dark purple dots in the yellow center. Let the pillowcase sit overnight before using.

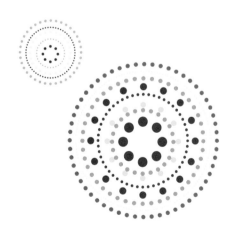

TIP Flowers not your thing? That's OK, this technique can be used to create almost anything that you can think of. The only limitation is your imagination!

Bleach Pen Jeans

Embellish these jeans with hearts, flowers, your initials—whatever you like!

SKILL LEVEL

Beginner

MATERIALS

Cardboard

Jeans

Bleach pen

Scrap fabric

Hydrogen peroxide

TO MAKE THE JEANS

1. Slip a piece of cardboard inside the jeans to prevent the bleach from soaking through. Practice drawing with the bleach pen on a piece of scrap fabric. Apply steady pressure to get an even line. When you feel confident, draw your design on the jeans.

2. When you're finished, let the jeans sit for 1 hour or so. Rinse with cold water, then pour hydrogen peroxide over the bleached portion. Let sit for 1 hour, then launder.

TIP Want to get a very fine line? Use a squeeze bottle with a metal tip (available in craft stores).

resources

DHARMA TRADING CO.

www.dharmatrading.com

Bleach-Stop, Synthrapol detergent, cotton clothing, and home items perfect for dying

CLOROX®

www.clorox.com

Bleach and bleach pens

TULIP®

www.tiedyeyoursummer.com

Dyes

RIT

www.ritstudio.com

Dyes and dye fixatives

JACQUARD

www.jacquardproducts.com/dyes

Crafting supplies, dyes, fabric, and paints

MICHAELS®

www.michaels.com

Crafting supplies, dyes, and items that are perfect for bleaching or dying

WALMART®

www.walmart.com

Crafting supplies, dyes, fabric, and markers

JO-ANN STORES℠

www.joann.com

Crafting supplies, dyes, and fabric

A.C. MOORE

www.acmoore.com

Crafting supplies and dyes

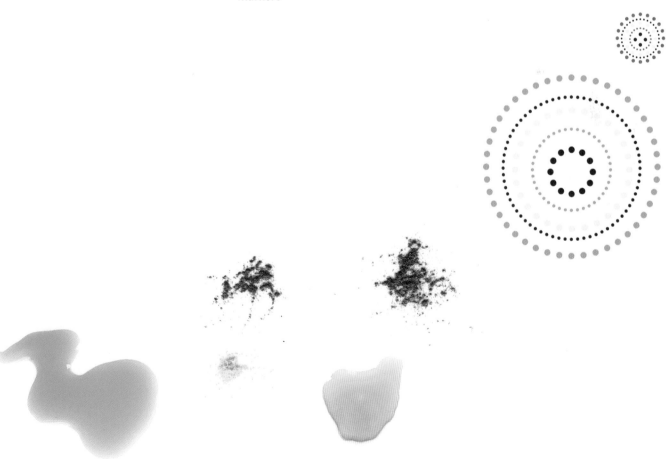

Look for these other *Threads* Selects booklets at www.tauntonstore.com and wherever crafts are sold.

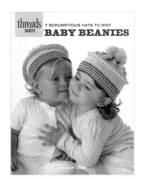

Baby Beanies
Debby Ware

EAN: 9781621137634
8½ x 10⅞, 32 pages
Product# 078001
$9.95 U.S., $9.95 Can.

Fair Isle Flower Garden
Kathleen Taylor

EAN: 9781621137702
8½ x 10⅞, 32 pages
Product# 078008
$9.95 U.S., $9.95 Can.

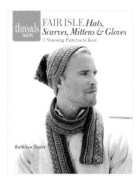

Fair Isle Hats, Scarves, Mittens & Gloves
Kathleen Taylor

EAN: 9781621137719
8½ x 10⅞, 32 pages
Product# 078009
$9.95 U.S., $9.95 Can.

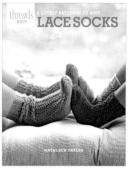

Lace Socks
Kathleen Taylor

EAN: 9781621137894
8½ x 10⅞, 32 pages
Product# 078012
$9.95 U.S., $9.95 Can.

Colorwork Socks
Kathleen Taylor

EAN: 9781621137740
8½ x 10⅞, 32 pages
Product# 078011
$9.95 U.S., $9.95 Can.

DIY Bride Cakes & Sweets
Khris Cochran

EAN: 9781621137665
8½ x 10⅞, 32 pages
Product# 078004
$9.95 U.S., $9.95 Can.

DIY Bride Beautiful Bouquets
Khris Cochran

EAN: 9781621137672
8½ x 10⅞, 32 pages
Product# 078005
$9.95 U.S., $9.95 Can.

Bead Necklaces
Susan Beal

EAN: 9781621137641
8½ x 10⅞, 32 pages
Product# 078002
$9.95 U.S., $9.95 Can.

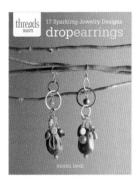

Drop Earrings
Susan Beal

EAN: 9781621137658
8½ x 10⅞, 32 pages
Product# 078003
$9.95 U.S., $9.95 Can.

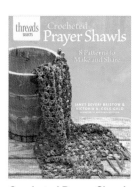

Crocheted Prayer Shawls
Janet Severi Bristow & Victoria A. Cole-Galo

EAN: 9781621137689
8½ x 10⅞, 32 pages
Product# 078006
$9.95 U.S., $9.95 Can.

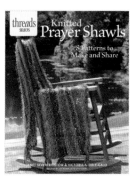

Knitted Prayer Shawls
Janet Severi Bristow & Victoria A. Cole-Galo

EAN: 9781621137696
8½ x 10⅞, 32 pages
Product# 078007
$9.95 U.S., $9.95 Can.

Shawlettes
Jean Moss

EAN: 9781621137726
8½ x 10⅞, 32 pages
Product# 078010
$9.95 U.S., $9.95 Can.

Easy-to-Sew Flowers
EAN: 9781621138259
8½ x 10⅞, 32 pages
Product# 078017
$9.95 U.S., $9.95 Can.

Easy-to-Sew Gifts
EAN: 9781621138310
8½ x 10⅞, 32 pages
Product# 078023
$9.95 U.S., $9.95 Can.

Easy-to-Sew Handbags
EAN: 9781621138242
8½ x 10⅞, 32 pages
Product# 078016
$9.95 U.S., $9.95 Can.

Easy-to-Sew Kitchen
EAN: 9781621138327
8½ x 10⅞, 32 pages
Product# 078024
$9.95 U.S., $9.95 Can.

Easy-to-Sew Lace
EAN: 9781621138228
8½ x 10⅞, 32 pages
Product# 078014
$9.95 U.S., $9.95 Can.

Easy-to-Sew Lingerie
EAN: 9781621138235
8½ x 10⅞, 32 pages
Product# 078015
$9.95 U.S., $9.95 Can.

Easy-to-Sew Pet Projects
EAN: 9781621138273
8½ x 10⅞, 32 pages
Product# 078018
$9.95 U.S., $9.95 Can.

Easy-to-Sew Pillows
EAN: 9781621138266
8½ x 10⅞, 32 pages
Product# 078019
$9.95 U.S., $9.95 Can.

**Easy-to-Sew
Scarves & Belts**
EAN: 9781621138211
8½ x 10⅞, 32 pages
Product# 078013
$9.95 U.S., $9.95 Can.

Easy-to-Sew Skirts
EAN: 9781621138280
8½ x 10⅞, 32 pages
Product# 078020
$9.95 U.S., $9.95 Can.

Easy-to-Sew Tote Bags
EAN: 9781621138297
8½ x 10⅞, 32 pages
Product# 078021
$9.95 U.S., $9.95 Can.

Easy-to-Sew Windows
EAN: 9781621138303
8½ x 10⅞, 32 pages
Product# 078022
$9.95 U.S., $9.95 Can.

If you like these projects, you'll love these other fun craft booklets.

Arm Knitting
Linda Zemba Burhance
EAN: 9781627108867,
8½ × 10⅞, 32 pages,
Product #078045, $9.95 U.S.

Fashionista Arm Knitting
Linda Zemba Burhance,
EAN: 9781627109567,
8½ × 10⅞, 32 pages,
Product # 078050, $9.95 U.S.

Bungee Band Bracelets & More
Vera Vandenbosch,
EAN: 9781627108898,
8½ × 10⅞, 32 pages,
Product # 078048, $9.95 U.S.

Mini Macrame
Vera Vandenbosch,
EAN: 9781627109574,
8½ × 10⅞, 32 pages,
Product # 078049, $9.95 U.S.

DecoDen Bling
Alice Fisher,
EAN: 9781627108874,
8½ × 10⅞, 32 pages,
Product # 078046, $9.95 U.S.

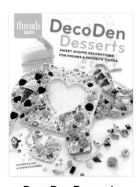

DecoDen Desserts,
Cathie Filian and Steve Piacenza,
EAN: 9781627109703,
8½ × 10⅞, 32 pages,
Product # 078053, $9.95 U.S.

Super Cute Duct Tape
Jayna Maleri,
EAN: 9781627109901,
8½ × 10⅞, 32 pages,
Product # 078056, $9.95 U.S.

Rubber Band Charm Jewelry
Maggie Marron,
EAN: 9781627108881,
8½ × 10⅞, 32 pages,
Product # 078047, $9.95 U.S.

Beautiful Burlap
Alice Fisher,
EAN: 9781627109888,
8½ × 10⅞, 32 pages,
Product # 078054, $9.95 U.S.

Shop for these and other great craft books and booklets online: www.tauntonstore.com

Simply search by product number or call 800-888-8286, use code MX800126
Call Monday-Friday 9AM – 9PM EST and Saturday 9AM – 5PM EST.
International customers, call 203-702-2204